Understanding
Psychometric
Testing
in a week

Understanding Psychometric Testing

in a week

**GARETH LEWIS AND
GENE CROZIER**

Hodder & Stoughton

A MEMBER OF THE HODDER HEADLINE GROUP

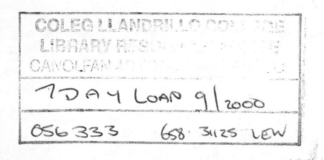
Orders: please contact Bookpoint Ltd, 39 Milton Park, Abingdon, Oxon OX14 4TD. Telephone: (44) 01235 400414, Fax: (44) 01235 400454. Lines are open from 9.00–6.00, Monday to Saturday, with a 24 hour message answering service. Email address: orders@bookpoint.co.uk

British Library Cataloguing in Publication Data
A catalogue record for this title is available from The British Library

ISBN 0 340 737808

First published 1999
Impression number   10 9 8 7 6 5 4 3 2
Year   2005 2004 2003 2002 2001 2000

Typeset by Multiplex Techniques Ltd, St Mary Cray, Kent.
Printed in Great Britain for Hodder & Stoughton Educational, a division of Hodder Headline Plc, 338 Euston Road, London NW1 3BH by Cox & Wyman Ltd, Reading, Berks.

○
ĭŊ the Institute
of Management

The Institute of Management (IM) is the leading organisation for professional management. Its purpose is to promote the art and science of management in every sector and at every level, through research, education, training and development, and representation of members' views on management issues.

This series is commissioned by IM Enterprises Limited, a subsidiary of the Institute of Management, providing commercial services.

Management House,
Cottingham Road,
Corby,
Northants NN17 1TT
Tel: 01536 204222;
Fax: 01536 201651
Website: http://www.inst-mgt.org.uk

Registered in England no 3834492
Registered office: 2 Savoy Court, Strand,
London WC2R 0EZ

CONTENTS

■ I N T R O D U C T I O N ■■

You may be one of the increasingly large numbers of people who have come across psychometric tests at work. As a manager, you may have used them for recruiting or selecting staff, or as part of a development or team-building programme. You may be a training or human-resource professional who has been involved in the use of such tests. Or, of course, you may well have been the subject of such testing yourself.

Alternatively, you may not have been involved in using such tests, but may have heard about them and what they can do. In any of these circumstances, you may have had some questions to ask. These might have included:

- 'What use will this be put to?'
- 'What can they tell about me?'
- 'What's actually in these tests?'
- 'Do the testers need to be qualified?'

and many more.

Psychometric testing, and the theory and practice that goes with it, can be quite complex and involved. It is perhaps not surprising that there are many misconceptions around. It is the purpose of this book to provide basic and simple descriptions of all aspects of psychometric tests and their use that will help anyone who is interested to get sensible answers to questions like those above. However, it is not a technical manual, and we have avoided bludgeoning the reader with highly technical or academic jargon. You don't need a degree in maths – or in any other subject – to read and understand the material in the book.

■ I N T R O D U C T I O N ■

The scope of the book covers:

Sunday	The importance of psychometric testing
Monday	What are psychometric tests?
Tuesday	Tests of ability and aptitude
Wednesday	What is personality?
Thursday	Selecting psychometric tests
Friday	The uses of psychometric tests
Saturday	The organisational perspective

The importance of psychometric testing

In this section, we aim to establish why psychometric testing is important. That it is increasingly seen as important is evidenced by the substantial growth in the use of psychometric tests in recent times.

To do this, we will consider:

- the human-relations approach to management
- the development of human-resource practices
- people, our greatest asset

The human-relations approach to management

Since the 1930s and the experiments of Elton Mayo at the Hawthorne Lighting factory, we have seen the development of the human-relations approach to management. We have developed an understanding that the motivation of workers is a key factor in their productivity at work. The importance of human relations as regards the success and productivity of organisations has now been well established, and accordingly the human relations movement has developed and matured. We now take it for granted that investment in people is as important as investment in other aspects of business or organisational life.

What is interesting is that although psychometric testing has been around for much of this century and has been widely available in many forms since the Second World War, it is only in the last few years that the growth has begun to accelerate.

Many of us, particularly in management or senior technical or professional positions, are likely to have encountered psychometric testing in some form. Despite this, there are still many misconceptions about what psychometric tests are and what their potential is in many areas of organisational and personal development.

Environmental influences
What are the influences that have stimulated the growth in testing? The broader influences on organisations include:

- managing change
- competitiveness
- downsizing
- a focus on productivity, and therefore on performance measurement
- a focus on creativity/team-building, and thus on personal behaviour and skills

As we move through what we have called the human-relations phase into the millennium, priorities are changing. This is the information age, and along with it is developing the knowledge economy. This will surely see an increase in the importance of the skills, capabilities and knowledge that people hold. In fact, the meaning of the knowledge economy is precisely that the knowledge and skills of individuals and organisations will be tradeable; and for many organisations, these factors will be the most important or their only asset.

Any organisation in such a position will want to defend its knowledge and skills. But before it can do that, it will need to know what it has got. This will involve an assessment and measurement of things that we have not traditionally been good at assessing and measuring. However, this is where psychometric testing can play a part.

The growth of testing
More specifically, some changes that have had a direct impact on the need for testing include the following:

1 Testing itself has become more sophisticated, with many more tests and suppliers of tests within the market.
2 Increased mobility in the job market, allied to a greater understanding of the cost of making the wrong appointment, has led to a search for more 'intelligent' tools to assess people for recruitment purposes.
3 A substantially greater priority has been given to learning and development in many organisations. This includes a greater need to assess people in terms of strengths, weaknesses and development needs, and psychometric tests have proved useful in doing this.

4 There has been a movement toward assessment as part of performance management.
5 The professionalisation of the human-resource function has occurred.
6 An understanding of the importance of personal skills, and of the influence of personal behaviour preferences on these, has also developed.
7 There have been changes in the 'contract' between organisation and employee that encompass much more than just the exchange of labour for money.

The development of human-resource practices

Alongside these more general organisational developments, and in healthy organisations at the centre of them, is the Human Resources (HR) function. In parallel with such developments, the HR function has developed many of its practices as part of its contribution to organisational development and success. A number of these are relevant to the present discussion. Some of these include:

• dealing with problems in selection
• quality assurance and development processes
• the movement towards competence

Dealing with problems in selection
For most of our working lifetimes, *the curriculum vitae (CV)*, along with the interview has been the stock-in-trade factor in selection. Yet there is a wealth of evidence that this process is flawed. Consider just some of the following points.

It has been shown that:

- interviewers make up their mind about a candidate from first impressions and then seek to justify that judgement
- judgements are often based on less-than-rational grounds – like appearance, gender, accent etc.
- few interviewers have appropriate training or skills for the job
- even well-conducted interviews, according to the British Psychological Society, are only 25 per cent better than choosing someone by sticking a pin in a list of candidates

So what we see is a collection of first impressions, negative information, self-delusion on the part of interviewers and a susceptibility to stereotypes. All of these limitations stem from the fact that the data is entirely subjective.

Once it is recognised that such selection processes are flawed, HR professionals need to identify more rational and effective ways to carry them out. Not least of the reasons for doing this is the cost of getting it wrong. Many costing exercises have been done, and of course the costs involved differs according to many of the circumstances involved. However, for a senior position it is not at all difficult to calculate that a poor appointment can cost upwards of £100,000 when the indirect as well as the direct costs are taken into account. This means quite clearly that it is massively cheaper to do it right first time – even if the direct and immediate costs are higher.

Psychometric testing has an important role to play in good selection procedures. Of course, it is not the whole answer, but tests have a great deal to contribute to robust and effective repertoires of assessment procedures. We shall discuss this in more detail on Thursday.

Quality-assurance and development processes
Training has always been important to most organisations. But more recently, we have seen a broader appreciation of the wider development perspective, and the need to see this as a process. This helps to ensure that development transfers to the working environment and that individual and team development are aligned with business priorities.

This approach is well exemplified in the Investors in People (IIP) initiative. This is a quality standard that underwrites the effectiveness of the development processes within an organisation. Although, of course, not all organisations have 'signed up' to IIP, it has been very influential in spreading the word about robust approaches to development.

The model of the process it espouses is as shown in the diagrams.

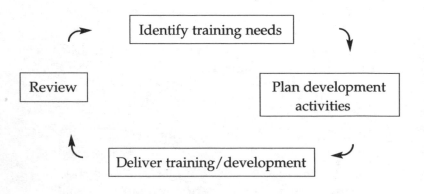

The Investors in People training model

You can recognise this as a typical quality process. However, one of the effects of the widespread knowledge and use of such a model is an increasing focus not just on getting the training done but also on making it 'intelligent'. By that we mean that development activities should be based on a thorough understanding of individual needs.

The knock-on consequence of this is that people need good information in order to understand and articulate development needs. This in turn puts the emphasis on means of assessment – everything from performance to ability to behavioural preferences – which is exactly where psychometric tests can often help.

The movement to competence

Organisations are increasingly using the notion of 'competence' as a language to describe the skills that underwrite their organisational development. In fact, there are two separate but related terms to consider here: competences and 'competencies'. Competences are output based and are 'can do' descriptions of the roles and tasks required in doing a particular job effectively. Competencies are more 'to have' descriptions of the fluid intelligences and their associated behaviour. They are the input side of the equation, and represent the underlying capabilities and characteristics that enable us to deliver on the competences.

People are our greatest asset

By way of a summary, we can extract from much of the reasoning and evidence above the simple statement: 'People are our greatest asset.'

What we value most about people at work is the knowledge and skills that they apply to that work. As we have said above, there is an increasing focus on the competencies that help people to deliver at work. These are sometimes explicitly called competencies, but they are also referred to as *personal effectiveness*. Some of the 'core' skills of personal effectiveness which seem to be most sought after include:

- teamworking
- leadership
- interpersonal skills
- management skills
- managing change
- customer skills
- managing self
- lifelong learning and development

The competence approach, particularly when the focus is on competencies, lends itself very well to measurement and evaluation. And as we have already pointed out, to assess and measure is one of the main drivers of interest in psychometric testing.

Summary

We have seen today that major changes in the environment in which organisations operate are forcing further substantial changes on them in order for them to remain competitive, healthy and successful. Many of the main HR practices have changed as a result of those pressures. This has involved a higher level of scrutiny on how we recruit, retain, manage and develop staff.

We have described trends that involve an increasing focus on competencies, or personal effectiveness, in an environment where assessment and measurement are seen as the best means of evaluating these. This is why you can see more use of psychometric tests at the moment, and why you will see even more in times to come. Tomorrow, we will look a little closer at the nature of the tests themselves.

What are psychometric tests?

This is an important question because there is much confusion as to what exactly makes a test psychometric. One particular misconception is that only tests that give us information about personality are in fact psychometric. This is not true, for the term can be applied to a much wider class of test.

Similarly, this begs the question as to what are the defining characteristics of such a test. Or, to put it another way: what does a test have to be to be called psychometric?

To answer these and other questions today, we will consider:

- the history of psychometric testing
- what puts the 'psycho' in psychometric
- what puts the 'metric' in psychometric
- interpreting test results

The history of psychometric testing

It is fairly natural and human to make judgements about the behaviour or potential of other people. This has been done throughout history, and as individuals we probably carry on this tradition ourselves. Just think of those people who may have made judgements about you over the years. Your list might include:

- parents and relatives
- friends
- teachers

- workmates
- managers and potential employers

However, on the whole, these judgements will most likely have been either subjective or based on flawed or incomplete information.

The first person to take a more systematic or 'scientific' approach to measuring some aspect of human behaviour or capability was a French psychologist called Binet. Binet was interested in the differences between children who achieved through education and those who did not, and he sought to be able to identify and measure those differences.

The focus of his interest was on those skills, including judgement, comprehension and ability to reason, which he felt distinguished achievers from non-achievers. He invented the term 'intelligence quotient' (IQ) to describe these characteristics, and he went on to develop a test to measure them objectively. Over the years, and for various reasons, the notion of IQ has been somewhat discredited, but today we are able to measure, by testing, a number of similar or related concepts.

The first major users of such tests were the military in the USA, but since the Second World War psychometric testing has moved both to education and to organisational life in general. The main difference today is that we can now measure a much broader range of characteristics using a comprehensive range of sophisticated instruments.

What puts the 'psycho' in psychometric?

Although there are many definitions, the British Psychological Society describes a psychometric test as: 'an instrument designed to produce a quantitative assessment of some psychological attribute or attributes'. 'Some psychological attribute' is a good description, but it doesn't tell us too much!

An alternative definition talks about: ' ... a capacity, propensity or liability to act, react, experience or to structure or order thought or behaviour in particular ways'.

In general, psychometric tests tend to relate to two distinct (but overlapping) kinds of performance:

1 Maximum performance
Tests here relate to our capacity or capability to do certain things. They include tests of intelligence, aptitude or ability. We will describe the full range of such tests tomorrow. For now, it is worth noting that they typically:

- have right and wrong answers
- measure the ability or achievement under strict conditions
- involve a certain level of difficulty so that performance can be compared from person to person

2 Habitual performance

This is also sometimes called 'typical performance', and tests here involve attempts to measure characteristic ways of behaving. They can also involve a consideration of how we perceive the world, and of attitudes, values and interests.

These tests:

- are self-descriptive
- indicate the most typical behaviour or preferences
- don't involve right or wrong answers

They are sometimes also referred to as 'psychological tests' or 'personality tests'. Interestingly, it is a common mistake for people to assume that it is just these (rather than the ability tests also) that are 'psychometric'.

We will discuss these tests in much more detail on Wednesday.

What puts the 'metric' in psychometric?

Clearly, as the name implies, this has something to do with measurement. It is primarily the fact that we are measuring and quantifying attributes that distinguishes psychometric testing from subjective judgement. However, developing a test is a whole process, and one which involves a number of components.

So there are a number of criteria that enable us to classify a test as psychometric. These include the following:

- It is constructed according to psychometric principles
- It is administered in a standardised way
- It is scored in a standardised way
- It is interpreted in a standardised way

How tests are developed

Most tests are of the pencil-and-paper type and consist of questions – or items, as they are called – and the basic process of constructing a test involves:

1 generating a large number of items;
2 the piloting and selection of items. This is done on the basis of a number of statistical tests which are described below;
3 standardising the scores. This enables raw scores to be translated into comparative scores;
4 writing the technical manual.

This process should be available to users of all robust tests, and should contain information both about the relevant statistics and about the appropriate administration, scoring and interpreting of the test.

Items for tests

For *ability* tests, like tests of intelligence, items can take various forms. Here are some examples:

- Analogy:
  Sparrow is to bird as minnow is to ...
  a) animal   b) ant   c) fish   d) bird   e) reptile

- Odd man out:
  24   63   10   48   35
- Sequences:
  8   11   14   17 ...

For most purposes, items are multi-choice, with only one right answer. However, there are variations, such as matching items.

For *personality* tests, there are a number of possibilities:

- *Dual response:* like 'yes/no' or 'true/false'. A variation on this is where a third, interim category is added, e.g. 'yes/not sure/no'; 'mostly/sometimes/never'; 'agree/uncertain/false'.
- *Rating scales:* where words on a continuum are each associated with a number, e.g.:
  Always..............often..............sometimes..............never
     1   2   3   4
- *forced choice:* sometimes called *ipsative*. Here, subjects are forced to choose, usually from a pair of words, which one most applies to them.

Selecting and testing items

There are a number of statistical tests that the items and the test as a whole should pass, and we will provide here a brief (and not too technical) overview which should give you an idea of the important considerations and questions to ask.

The two basic concepts that are involved are:

1 validity
2 reliability

Validity

A test is valid if it measures what it says it measures. This is a simple starting point, but validity can be a complex topic. There are a number of facets to it, and thus a number of different ways of describing, measuring and demonstrating validity. The most important are:

- *face validity:* this is the extent to which the test appears to the user to test the attribute in question. Its main value is in gaining co-operation from test takers.
- *construct validity:* the question here is whether the test fully describes the variable being measured.
- *content validity:* this answers the question 'Does this test measure all aspects of the variable in question?'
- *criterion-related validity:* this establishes the predictive value of the test: whether it can predict some measured, real-world criterion. In general, this is quite difficult to achieve to a high degree. However, where it can be justified, it is obviously very powerful.

Reliability

Reliability has two distinct meanings. A test is reliable if it is self-consistent, that is, its various parts are measuring the same thing. A good test should also give the same score for each subject (as long as their ability has not changed) when they are retested. This is called *test–retest reliability*.

Reliability is also important in influencing the validity factor: valid tests are also *consistent* ones.

Whenever you are faced with choices about using tests, you should ask searching questions about the reliability and validity of a test. As a user, you need to be reassured by its robustness and effectiveness.

Administering tests

The results of a test are meaningful and reliable only if everyone takes it in the same conditions. This can be illustrated by a very simple example. Suppose you want to test a group of people using a numerical-ability test. You could just hand the test out and ask the subjects to return it in the next few days. However, there would be a few disadvantages to this:

- They might 'crib' the answers
- They would be doing the test in different conditions and environments
- They would take different amounts of time to do the test

If any or all of these are the case, then we would not be comparing apples with apples.

In the case of an ability test, the time to answer might be an important part of the variable being measured, which is why many ability tests are timed.

To get over these problems, test suppliers should supply a user manual which describes the test administration in some detail, including the actual script to be spoken.

For the reasons outlined above, it is important that these instructions be kept to precisely.

Interpreting test results

If a subject scores 20 out of 25 on a verbal-reasoning test, what does this mean? A first response might be to say that because they have scored more than half, that must be a good result. But, on the other hand, doesn't it depend on how 'difficult' the test is?

It is for this reason that raw scores on a test are always converted into a 'profile score' which compares the score for this subject with the scores of some known group of people. This process is called *standardising the scores*. It works as follows.

As with most variables that occur in the natural world, measurements for a population are distributed in a characteristic way. For instance, if we measured the heights of a large and representative sample of the population and put these on a *frequency diagram*, they would look as shown in the diagram. The shape of this line occurs so often that it has been given a name: the 'normal distribution'. It is bell-shaped and symmetrical, and the average (or mean) is the highest point on the curve.

Another statistic which is very relevant in this distribution is called the 'standard deviation' (SD). This is the square root of the average distance of the scores from the mean, and it measures the spread of the distribution. Its main advantage is that we can work out the proportion of people who score above or below any particular standard-deviation score. For instance, we know that 68 per cent of people will score between plus and minus 1 SD score (the area shown on the diagram below). When raw scores are converted into standardised scores, each score is placed in relation to the rest of the population. There are two popular ways of doing this:

1 *sten (standard ten) scores:* these 'carve' the distribution up into 10 units, with the middle being at 5.5 – see the figure

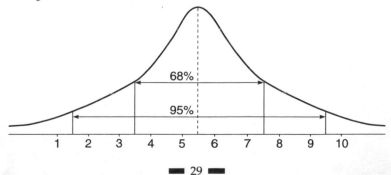

2 *percentiles:* these carve the distribution up into 100 units, with the middle being at 50.

A question worth asking with the standardised scores used for any test is: what is the group or population against which I am being compared? A percentile score, on an ability test, of 60 (which means a score higher than 60 per cent of the population) is one thing if you are being compared with the population *as a whole*. However, if you are being compared to just a graduate or a senior-management population, then the interpretation will be slightly different.

Summary

Because for many people, the 'technical' aspect of test design and interpretation is the most difficult – both because it is quite complex, and even more so because it can be very mathematical – we shall summarise today's work. This is because, although there are some complex ideas here, behind them are some simple but important things to remember.

- The 'science' of testing means not only that tests are systematically designed, but also that there are measures of important aspects of tests that you should ask about and pay attention to
- Amongst these, information about reliability and validity are the most important
- Tests should be administered and scored in a standardised way, according to the instructions
- Scores are made meaningful by being converted into standardised scores which compare a result with some population
- The most usual ways to do this are by using sten scores or percentiles

Finally, of course, in many circumstances we will give feedback on results to subjects. However, we will cover this in more detail on Friday.

Tests of ability and aptitude

Yesterday, we made the distinction between tests of maximum performance and tests of habitual or typical performance. It is the former that are the tests of ability and aptitude, and these we shall focus on in more detail today. Specifically, we shall look at:

- the concept of intelligence
- types of test
- guidelines for selecting and using tests

The concept of intelligence

We need to consider this topic because, as we have explained, it is at the heart of the development of psychometric testing. Many of the reasons that made it of interest at the turn of the last century are just as valid today. Although the language and the degree of sophistication of the testing process have changed, it is still just as important.

Binet's approach to intelligence, as already mentioned, was expressed in terms of the intelligence quotient (IQ). This expressed the ratio of the mental age to the chronological age, and was based around an average of 100. Because it related intelligence to development, and its primary focus was children, the measure was not appropriate when applied to adults. However, the concept was nonetheless considered to be important. Having said that, we also need to understand that it has been remarkably difficult to define the concept without colliding with different cultural definitions as to what constitutes intelligence.

What we do know is that the ability to perform certain types of task successfully means that it is more likely that we can also perform other, similar types of task successfully. Thus, psychologists have postulated such a thing as 'general intelligence'. Intelligence has been described by Spearman as the quality that allows people to do well on most tasks. This is seen as the 'driving force' behind many of the more specific abilities that we recognise and which we can measure. This description does suggest some types of continuum:

Generalised intelligence/ability ←——→ Specific skills

Potential to act ←————→ Real actions/behaviour

Far from job ←————————→ Near to job

This demonstrates that either we can seek to look at the underlying capability or we can focus on specific skills that are known to be of interest. It is the particular context that will dictate which of these (or both) is of most interest.

Types of test

We have already described that the early history of testing was focused on the generalised notion of intelligence. However, it soon grew from there. The recognition of the complex nature of ability, and of the continuum which moves from the very general to the highly specific, widened out the scope of interest. Any ability that humans can use or express, and any behaviour that they undertake, can in principle be tested for. This means that there is an astonishing range of possible candidates for testing. As a general guide, it is worth following the dictum that anything that can be tested almost certainly *has* been. In this section, we shall describe and illustrate some of the major categories of test.

Before we look in detail at some types of test, we should remark that ability tests do have some characteristics that set them apart from the personality tests that we shall discuss tomorrow. These include:

- They are not self-assessed
- They involve right–wrong answers (with certain exceptions)
- They are administered in rigorous circumstances, particularly in selection and recruitment procedures
- They are often timed

In general, there are three classes of test:

1 *objective ability tests* – which test general intellectual functions, or more specific abilities

2 *achievement tests* – like reading, clerical coding and
   basic operator skills
3 *performance tests* – like standardised work-sample tests.

General ability tests
These test underlying cognitive ability and mental
functioning. Typical of these are tests of verbal and
numerical reasoning. Many test suppliers supply tests with
both these components, and sometimes a third component,
abstract reasoning, is also added. Such collections are called
'batteries' of tests. A battery of tests is a collection of tests
that together give a rounded picture of the psychological
attributes sought by the tester.

A typical battery is the GRT series by Psytech which
provides verbal, numerical and abstract tests at both
general and graduate levels. Typical (but not actual) items
look like this:

- *Verbal:* designed to test an understanding of words and of relationships between words.
  Dark means the opposite of?

1	2	3	4	5	6
gloomy	happy	red	heavy	light	day

- *Numeric:* designed to assess the ability to work with numbers.
  4 is to 12 as 8 is to?

1	2	3	4	5	6
16	24	20	64	32	36

- *Abstract:* designed to assess relationships between shapes and figures.

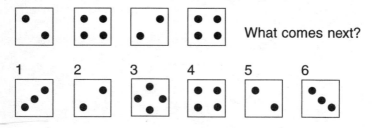

What comes next?

It should also be borne in mind that tests and test batteries should be sensitised to the level of the takers. In this way, the AH series of tests is differentiated by ability. AH4, 3 and 2 are suitable for the general population, whilst AH5 and 6 are suitable for a graduate population.

The Raven Progressive Matrices is another well-known test which exists in standard and advanced versions.

Other ability tests
Some tests involve knowledge or achievement as well as ability. Examples might include tests of:

- mechanical reasoning or mechanical comprehension
- critical thinking ability

An example of the above is the Watson-Glaser Critical Thinking Appraisal. This tests for a range of critical reasoning abilities like:

- the ability to draw inferences
- the recognition of assumptions
- deduction
- interpretation
- the evaluation of arguments

For example:
Statement:
Some holidays are rainy. All rainy days are boring.
Therefore:
Proposed conclusions (Yes/No)

1 No clear days are boring
2 Some holidays are boring
3 Some holidays are not boring

Occupational ability tests
Even more specific in their analysis of abilities, these tests have been developed for particular jobs or quite specific applications. Examples include tests for:

- programming
- computer operations
- word processing
- foreign-language learning
- clerical aptitude
- manual dexterlty
- hand–eye co-ordination

Skills and knowledge tests

These can take a number of forms. They can be targeted at basic skills such as reading, arithmetic, oral communication and so on. Alternatively, they can be targeted at more specific job-related skill areas such as clerical, typing and other operator skills. Where they are related to a knowledge base, they typically seek not just knowledge of facts but also an ability at judgement and decision-making in using the knowledge base.

An example of an applied judgement test is the Management Self Assessment Test (MSAT) developed by the Institute of Management. This is a self-assessment test which covers important elements of required managerial knowledge and judgement. Thus, it gives an indication of the level of performance in a management role. It looks at:

- general managerial knowledge and judgement
- the ability to conceptualise typical management problems and solutions
- the ability to think critically and logically in solving those problems

It involves 70 questions based on 7 realistic management scenarios or case studies. Here is a sample item:

1. In Arab countries during Ramadan, good Muslims do not eat during the day but only after sundown and before sunrise. An expatriate Western manager has found it commercially profitable to give key account clients a buffet lunch when making marketing presentations. During Ramadan, what should he do?

   a) skip the food

b) have food in another room for non-Muslims
c) give the presentation and lunch in the evening
d) make no change in his routine

What is involved in developing skills and knowledge tests?
Developing job-specific tests may be attractive, but just
what is involved and how much does it cost? To develop
MSAT, the Institute of Management needed to satisfy three
requirements:

1 possession of specialist expertise in test design and
   validation
2 access to a group of subject-matter experts
3 the opportunity to test the items on a representative
   sample of managers.

The test itself was designed over a period of six months
using about 20 subject-matter experts. Most of the time was
taken up reviewing and editing items. In this first stage, a
pool of managers from different organisations was used to
review and test the individual items. Once the test had
been designed, field trials were carried out to prove the test
worked. The test was applied to over 1,500 managers in a
variety of organisations. Some items which had appeared
okay in the early trials soon revealed problems, and the test
had to be adjusted. Once the final format for the test had
been decided, samples had to be analysed to demonstrate
the link between the test results and job performance (in
this case, the level of management). This stage took more
than six months.

All this took slightly more than one year to complete. In staff terms, it required a significant commitment from one senior manager, specialist expertise from one occupational psychologist and support from a significant number of companies.

Job performance tests
Performance tests have been developed for many craft and technical jobs. As well as current ability, they can also focus on the ability to learn in real work situations.

Guidelines for selecting and using tests

In this section, we shall gather some thoughts about how to use ability tests in practice.

1 *Start with the job.* As always with assessment exercises, it is necessary to have a detailed description of the

required skills. The abilities, aptitudes, skills and knowledge required for the application should be well defined and based on a sound knowledge of the job under discussion. Test data will not provide you with good information if you do not know the standards you are seeking.

You also need to set criteria relating to the results. Are you comparing competitively with other job holders/subjects? Are you comparing with the norms? Are you comparing with some preset standard?

2 *Use batteries of tests*. In most real situations, a single test may not give wide or comprehensive data across all of the target abilities. Thus, you may need to use a number of tests that provide this range of data. Alternatively, you can use one of the batteries mentioned above or in the digest below to get the required coverage.

3 *Evaluate the proposed tests*. Look at the test supplier's data on reliability and validity. Check if the test/battery is levelled appropriately for your target audience. You might also want to gain some third-party or objective opinion, such as the excellent BPS reviews we discuss on Thursday. Alternatively, check with your trade association, or better still, find someone who has used the tests in practice.

4 *Get expert help*. You might use consultants at any or all points in the process:

- to advise on test choice
- to be a licensed purchaser
- to add objectivity to the process
- to administer and interpret professionally

5 *Use results in conjunction with other data.* This is a general rule which makes a lot of sense. We shall talk in more detail about these other kinds of data in the following days.

The list of test suppliers in the appendix or your professional association are good starting points for tracking down relevant and useful tests.

Summary

Today, we have looked at the whole field of aptitude and ability testing. We have examined the whole range of abilities, skills and attributes that the different tests can measure. We have also looked at their applicability to the organisational context. You should now have some appreciation of some of the major ability tests and what they do.

Tomorrow, we move on to examine the much more complex notion of personality and the associated tests.

What is personality?

In the past three days, you have examined the purpose of
psychometric tests and the way they are designed and
validated, as well as reviewed some of the main types.
Today we are going to examine one of the most important
and perhaps controversial uses of these tests: to gain an
insight into the personalities of test-takers. Before we
review the applications available to organisations and
managers, we shall spend some time studying the nature of
personality.

By the time you have finished this section, you should have
a clear idea of what personality tests can or cannot do, and
be ready to examine the various applications for
psychometric tests in organisations on Friday.

What do we mean by personality?

Ask 20 psychologists to define personality and you will get
20 different answers. What they generally mention,
however, is an individual's characteristic patterns of
thinking, feeling and acting across a wide range of
situations. What are the consistent features of the way they
behave? What makes them unique? Already here we have
the concepts of consistency and repetition, implying that
aspects of personality can be measured).

The development of modern personality theory

Interest in measuring an individual's psychology can be

traced back to the Second World War when the need to recruit large numbers of men into the armed forces led to the development of mental aptitude tests in the USA and Britain. Personality testing really did not get off the ground until after the war, although the theory behind these tests was developed by Allport in the 1930s.

Research into the nature of personality has mainly focused on 'personality traits' and on 'typologies'.

Personality traits
Modern theories of personality can still be traced back to the early work of Galton from 1869 onwards. Galton was interested in the nature of genius, and began his work by reviewing all the words we use to describe personality (the lexicon approach). He then attempted to group these descriptions into a classification scheme. Allport continued this work in the 1930s, but it was only after the Second World War that the scientific measurement of personality really came into being with the work of Cattell.

Cattell began by asking individuals to rate each other using the descriptions of personality used in everyday language. His review of the data suggested that there were no more than about 50 underlying dimensions. Further work with larger samples and the advanced statistical techniques pioneered by Spearman led to his conclusions that there were no more than 12 Life (L) factors involved. Cattell then began to devise questionnaire items to measure these 12 factors and subsequently identified a further 4 factors (Q) from an analysis of the questionnaire returns.

The 16 primary factors identified by Cattell and now contained in the 16PF test are as follows:

A Warmth	L Vigilance
B Reasoning	M Abstractness
C Emotional stability	N Privateness
E Dominance	O Apprehension
F Liveliness	Q1 Openness to change
G Rule-consciousness	Q2 Self-reliance
H Social boldness	Q3 Perfectionism
I Sensitivity	Q4 Tension

Each factor is measured on a spectrum expressed as word pairs, e.g. *Warmth* is measured on a scale of *Reserved–Warm*.

Factor analysis
One of the key tools in this research was 'factor analysis', which at its time was a revolutionary technique. Now it is a standard tool used by psychology students all over the

world. Fortunately, we do not need to worry about the mathematics involved!

In simple terms, factor analysis studies the correlations between the variables in complex data sets containing many variables (multivariate analysis) and patterns of variation (variance) in the data. Computer programs attempt to distinguish between independent variation in each variable and the variation that can be explained by common unidentified factors linking the different variables. The final output is a list of equations for a series of common factors linked to a figure for the amount of variation in the data set that can be explained by the existence of each factor. Psychologists can then study the nature of these patterns and formulate models for the factors explaining human behaviour.

Cattell used factor analysis to identify the primary factors in his questionnaire.

How personality tests are designed
A personality test is simply a series of questions that assess an individual's thinking, feeling and acting in different situations. Typically these questions will ask you how much you agree or disagree with a statement on a five-point scale, e.g.

I think personality tests are a load of nonsense

strongly agree	agree	not sure	disagree	strongly disagree
O	O	O	O	O

or they ask the test-taker to choose between options, e.g.:

When relaxing, I would prefer to:

(a) listen to some classical music
(b) go and play a game of squash
(select option a or b)

A key feature of these tests is that they measure your stated preferences (often referred to as 'self reports') and are not trying to uncover some hidden part of your nature you would rather cover over. In this respect, they are quite different from the use of handwriting tests, where a single interpreter seeks to identify 'hidden' aspects of your personality from a sample of hand-writing.

Jungian typology
The theory of psychological types was developed by Carl Jung (1875–1961) to explain some of the apparently random differences in people's behaviour. Following extensive work on clients and others, Jung discovered predictable and differing patterns of behaviour. His theory of personality types recognised the existence of distinct patterns and provided an explanation for how these types develop.

According to Jung, differences in behaviour are caused by differences in the way people like to use their minds. The central idea is that when your mind is active, you are involved in one of two key mental activities:

1 taking information in, i.e. *Perceiving*, or
2 organising that information internally and coming to conclusions, i.e. *Judging*.

In turn, Jung observed that there were two opposite ways of *Perceiving*, which he called *Sensing* and *Intuition*, and two opposite ways of *Judging*, which he called *Thinking* and *Feeling*. Everyone uses these essential processes on a daily basis, both towards the external world of people, things and events (*Extraversion*) and towards the inner world of ideas, thought and reflection (*Introversion*). These four basic processes provide you with eight different ways of using your mind.

Jung believed that everyone has a natural preference for using one kind of Perceiving and one kind of Judging, and he observed that each was drawn towards either the external or internal world. This idea was later expanded by Katherine Cook Briggs and her daughter, Isabel Briggs Myers, and used to develop the Myers-Briggs Type Indicator (MBTI) instrument.

Today the Myers-Briggs Type Inventory (MBTI) is one of the most widely used personality tests, and has been translated into a number of languages. It can provide considerable insight into the way an individual relates to others, and into their preferred team role and work environment.

The MBTI is based on Jung's typology, and reports your preference on four scales, each consisting of two opposite poles:

1 *Extraversion or Introversion (E–I)*: where you prefer to focus your attention;
2 *Sensing or Intuition (S–N)*: the way you prefer to take in information;
3 *Thinking or Feeling (T–F)*: the way you prefer to make decisions;
4 *Judging or Perceiving (J–P)*: the way you orientate yourself to the outside world.

Combinations of these four scales give us 16 different types as shown below. Each type can be referred to by a four-letter code.

	ST: Sensing-Thinking	SF: Sensing-Feeling
IJ–Introvert-Judging	ISTJ	ISFJ
IP–Introvert-Perceiving	ISTP	ISFP
EP–Extravert-Perceiving	ESTP	ESFP
EJ–Extravert-Judging	ESTJ	ESFJ
	NF: Intuitive-Feeling	NT: Intuitive-Thinking
IJ–Introvert-Judging	INFJ	INTJ
IP–Introvert-Perceiving	INFP	INTP
EP–Extravert-Perceiving	ENFP	ENTP
EJ–Extravert-Judging	ENFJ	ENTJ

Many managers fall into the ESTJ type. Here is an abbreviated description of this type:

> *Practical, realistic and matter-of-fact with a natural ability for practical subjects like business or mechanics. They are not interested in abstract theories and expect their learning to have immediate and practical application. They love to organise and run activities. They are decisive, acting quickly to implement decisions and can be relied upon to pay attention to practical, routine issues.*

This seems to be a pretty good description of a typical

manager. Of course, this does not mean that the other types
make poor managers, and a quick review of the others will
highlight those types who make great leaders (e.g. ENTJ) or
entrepreneurs (e.g. INTJ).

Typologies have one great advantage: they are easy to
understand and to relate to. They are often a great tool for
developing individuals and for increasing their awareness
of some of their main patterns of behaviour and how others
see them. This approach also stresses a key principle about
the use of personality scales, namely that there is no right
or wrong preference. On the other hand, typologies are
generally less suited to selection because they are too
simplistic and do not allow us to discriminate clearly
between individuals.

The 'Big Five'
Sooner or later if you talk to anyone about personality tests,
you will hear them mention 'the Big Five'. These arose from
the work of Costa and McCrae in 1985 who studied the

results of a range of personality questionnaires using factor analysis and who identified 5 *big factors* that could explain most of the personality space covered by all these different measures. On the basis of this research, they designed the NEO-Personality Inventory which measures differences between individuals on these five dimensions as described below.

1. *Neuroticism:* high scorers here are generally more sensitive, emotional and prone to feelings that are upsetting such as guilt or sadness. Low scorers are emotionally secure, resistant and relaxed individuals even under very stressful conditions.

2. *Extraversion:* high scorers here are extraverted, outgoing, active and high-spirited. They prefer to be around people most of the time. Low scorers are introverted, reserved and serious. They prefer to be alone or with a few close friends.

3. *Openness to experience:* high scorers here are open to new experiences, with broad interests and a strong imagination. Low scorers are down-to-earth, practical, traditional and pretty much set in their ways.

4. *Agreeableness:* high scorers here are compassionate, good-natured and generally eager to co-operate and avoid conflict. Low scorers are hard-headed, sceptical, proud and competitive. They tend to express their anger directly and forcefully.

5. *Conscientiousness*: high scorers here are conscientious and well organised. They have high standards and always strive to achieve their goals. Low scorers are

easygoing, not very well organised and sometimes rather careless. They prefer not to make plans if they can help it.

In fact, these five factors can be related to the global factors found in multifactor tests like the 16PFV5 and 15FQ. They also link to the dimensions in the Jungian typology.

Sometimes the computer print outs from personality tests provide values for dimensions contained in other tests such as the Belbin Roles, Leadership and Subordinate Styles, and Jungian types. These are estimates provided by the test designers and should be treated with caution.

Since the publication of Costa and McCrae's work, the issue of the Big Five has attracted a lot of controversy, mainly on the grounds that they cannot cover all aspects of personality. However, a number of studies across a wide range of occupational groups have in fact shown correlations between ratings on these dimensions and job performance criteria.

Some key personality tests
- *16PF:* the original 16-factor test developed by Cattell that has spawned many similar 15–17 factor tests.
- *15FQ:* a similar instrument to the 16PF produced by Psytech International.
- *Belbin Team Roles:* popular due to availability of the questionnaire in the public domain, the Belbin test has its fans and critics. It does allow companies to combine personal development, team-building activities and job analysis within one activity.
- *Myers-Briggs Type Indicator (MBTI):* already discussed.
- *NEO-IP:* easy to administer and score, this questionnaire evaluates you against the Big Five factors.

- *OPQ:* the Occupational Personality Questionnaire is one of the best-known instruments, and is offered by Saville & Holdsworth.

Other well-known instruments include the California Personality Inventory (CPI), the Gordon Personal Profile Inventory, the Guilford-Zimmerman Temperament Survey and OPP.

Details of some of the main suppliers are provided at the end of this book.

The complex nature of personality
Personality and personal-values questionnaires are relatively cheap and easy to administer and score, but are certainly less reliable and valid than tests of mental ability. Little or no evidence of criterion validity (i.e. relevance to the job) has been found for many personality tests and scales. The fact that the questions themselves often have no relevance to the workplace does not help. In some well-documented cases, their value in selecting people from unusual backgrounds or different cultures has been questioned because test design is heavily influenced by culture.

This does not mean, however, that personality tests do not have an important role to play in organisations. But they must be used intelligently, and users need to recognise their limitations. Even a perfect test (if it existed!) can be misused, and most of the examples used to criticise the use of personality tests are due to *misuse of the test* and not to the *test design* itself. Administering the test is the easy part, but the minute a test user receives the results they enter a danger zone with many traps for the unwary. This is

because the two most important stages of test use –
interpretation and *using the results to make decisions* – are
profoundly influenced by the situation and may also be left
in the hands of those with insufficient expertise.

Misinterpretation of tests
Personality tests are very open to misinterpretation. Your
stated preference is just that: it does not mean you always
behave that way, and it does need to be placed in the
context of your experience, acquired skills and
environment. For example, if you are a strong introvert, this
does not mean that you are automatically shy, retiring and
unable to perform well in social situations. In reality, we all
acquire skills that enable us to perform well in areas that
may not be our natural preference. We know many
consultants who are seen as extreme extraverts but who are
actually the opposite, but their lifestyle and job has taught
them to behave as extraverts.

Inappropriate use of personality tests also leads people to
arrive at the wrong conclusions and to take bad decisions.
In selection, for example, you can only use the results of
tests successfully if you have shown key features of
personality to be critical to the job and have correctly
interpreted the results for individuals. Ultimately, the test-
taker is probably the best judge of the accuracy of the
report, which is why detailed feedback is usually advised.

Does your personality profile change?
Generally, the profiles of most individuals remain stable at
least over several years. However, they can be affected by
periods of change or stress, and this does need to be taken
into account. Over longer periods of time there is no doubt
that individuals may 'drift' on individual scales, usually

because they have learned new skills and ways of thinking.
People working in highly disciplined professions like the
law or science may develop profiles matching the job
requirements more closely. There seems to be some
evidence that some effective managers can develop more
balanced profiles as they increase their repertoire of
behavioural skills (notably in Introversion–Extraversion).

Summary

Today we have looked at the basic principles upon which personality tests are designed. We have learned that personality tests in general are focused on identifying individual preferences on a limited number of dimensions. We have also found that special care must be used in their interpretation, and that this, rather than any flaw in their design, is usually the source of problems.

Tomorrow, we shall turn our attention to some of the key issues surrounding the use of psychometric tests in organisations.

Selecting psychometric tests

Today, we look in more detail at what is involved in selecting and using tests within a recruitment and selection context. Specifically, we shall look at:

- the selection process
- reviewing the assessment methods available
- selecting the right tests
- the interpretation of test results

The selection process

Even if we know a psychometric test is reliable and valid, we can only exploit its full potential with an effective selection process. Most people can recall examples where candidates for a job have been exposed to a pretty gruelling procedure only to have all that effort wasted by one interviewer's prejudices. Before we can use a test, therefore, we must consider all aspects of the selection process.

Identifying job requirements
In most selection situations, it is useful to regard the selection process as a process that brings together all the information we gain about an applicant, in the form of an 'applicant profile'. This profile will not just contain information about their personality but will also include information on their abilities and aptitudes, their qualifications and training, and their experience, as well as any other general information relevant to the job in question. This applicant profile clearly relates to the concept of an ideal job profile or 'person specification',

which typically consists of a list of criteria matching our idealised impression of the job holder. Of course, this ideal rarely matches reality, so we are forced to discriminate between the *essential* and the *desirable,* and then to compare individual applicant profiles against this final profile.

If we are supplied with a good job spec, the task of producing the ideal applicant profile should be relatively easy. However, it is always worth reviewing the job spec in a wider context to ensure that it is based on reality, not just on optimistic goals, and is expressed in terms of the specific tasks required for the post. From these, we should be able to clearly identify the critical requirements for fulfilling the requirements of the job.

This is the theory at least, but typically, job specs are produced by line managers and may not be that accurate. It is important to recognise that effective recruitment and selection of the workforce should form just one part of an integrated strategy for improving the quality of the work-force with several key components as shown in the diagram.

Human-resource quality-improvement model

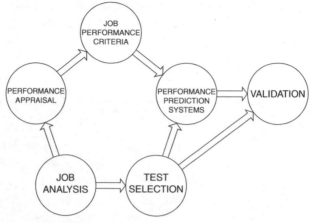

- *Job analysis* is the starting point, and can be achieved using several different techniques. Job-analysis interviews and questionnaires can identify the elements that are most relevant to different jobs. A more specialised approach is the use of Repertory Grid Analysis (RGA) or Critical Incident Analysis (CIA) to clarify the characteristics of successful job holders.
- *Performance appraisal systems* should of course reflect the key elements of a job identified by detailed job analysis. Staff need to be trained to implement the system in a consistent and reliable manner.
- *Job performance criteria* need to be identified that will allow the organisation to link assessment criteria (and therefore chosen tests) to job performance.
- *Performance prediction systems* will ultimately enable us to fine-tune human-resource planning and assessment techniques.
- *Validation* is of course the key to the system, and should seek to determine whether individuals selected under the

new system really do perform better than through previous procedures. One approach is to compare the performance of samples of employees selected under different systems.

Prioritising requirements

No recruitment and selection process can cover all aspects of human behaviour, nor is any one individual likely to fulfil all requirements. The importance of prioritising these requirements cannot be overemphasised. It is common for organisations to use a weighting scheme in the selection process (i.e. different dimensions are given different levels of importance), and although this may seem somewhat bureaucratic, the discussion of both the weightings and the results amongst the decision-makers is really what matters.

Reviewing the assessment methods available

Psychometric tests are just one method of assessing individuals. Their great advantage is their ease of use and low cost, but they do require access to the right sort of expertise and may have relatively low job relevance. Organisations should carry out a comprehensive review of all the methods available to them.

Here, with their advantages and disadvantages, are some of the options that should be considered when looking to balance psychometric data with other types of data:

- *Application form:* this is a method of collecting information at the early stages of the selection process. It is standardised in structure, but provides minimal data.

- *Curriculum vitae:* This is a method of evaluating career history and achievements. It can build up a good picture of a candidate, but it is not standardised and needs verifying.
- *References and testimonials:* this is third party data about an individual. At best can give a picture of a person's strengths through the eyes of a stakeholder. However, it is not standardised, and it is likely to be subjective.
- *Biodata:* this is biographical data based on forced choice questions. It can be very effective when standardised, objective and verified. However, it has to be custom designed and evaluated.
- *Biographical interview:* this is a structured interview covering education, achievements, interests, career and relationships. A more recent development is the competence-based interview which focuses on individual style and achievement in relation to a specific competence framework. The biographical interview produces high-quality data if structured appropriately. However, it needs a great deal of skill to construct and to conduct. It also needs an appropriate competence framework to underwrite it.
- *Records of qualification and achievement:* these are what as the name implies. They are objective and easily obtainable, but they are limited in scope.
- *Performance appraisal:* this comprises information about performance in the job; such appraisal adds some objective data from a range of stakeholders. A performance appraisal provides good data if conducted

reliably; and the 360-degree process can be particularly powerful. However, it is difficult to obtain or verify as a third party. It is also time consuming.

- *Assessment centre:* this involves candidates in a variety of activities and exercises, each of which is designed to provide data on different aspects of aptitude, skill and knowledge in terms of real behaviour in realistic situations. It produces a range of very powerful data on behaviour in realistic situations. However, it is also expensive and time consuming.
- *Interview:* already discussed, this provides first hand data and impressions of the person involved. However, and again as mentioned above, it is not very accurate, objective and reliable.

Here are some simple rules to guide your decisions as to different assessment methods:

- Rule One: always remember that many of the traditional methods used in selection are notoriously unreliable.
- Rule Two: if you are worried about the cost of applying a more rigorous approach to selection, try calculating the costs of a wrong decision.
- Rule Three: the attention paid to the assessment of individual dimensions should be in direct proportion to the importance of the dimension.
- Rule Four: the reliability and accuracy of the assessment increases rapidly when there are multiple assessments.
- Rule Five: always consider each job separately. You should not continue to use particular tests because the company 'has always dome it that way'.

Selecting the right tests

Every manager considering the optimum mix of tests to use within current constraints of time and resources is faced with a dilemma:

- Should they select or even design a specific test that gives a precise and highly reliable measurement of a limited but critical aspect of a job, or
- Should they use a variety of tests that are less precise and predictive, but which provide a broader and more comprehensive range of competencies?

CLOSING THE
SALE
APPRAISAL
TEST

Given the pace of change in the modern work environment, there is probably a tendency to use broader-based tools.

In the final analysis, test users should be committed to using only those tests which can be shown to meet the purpose for which they are to be used and that are appropriate for the intended test-takers. This means test users should:

- define the purpose of the testing, and identify the target population
- select a test that matches the purpose and population, based on a thorough review of all available information, including, where possible, independent test reviews
- read all the support materials provided by test developers, and avoid using tests where the information in these materials is unclear or incomplete
- ensure they become familiar with the background to the test's development, and that they understand the technical research data underpinning the test
- examine specimen materials, including questionnaires, test instructions, answer sheets, manuals, scored results and computer feedback reports, before selecting a test

This is clearly a rather rigorous process and a little off-putting. Small wonder that some organisations are inclined to cut corners and leave the decision to an expert. If you are tempted to do this, remind yourself that careless selection of tests has landed some large organisations in an industrial tribunal. At the very least, your selection process will be flawed and you can expect poorer results.

Checklist for selecting a test
Let's imagine that you have followed the process through and are about to make a final decision on the use of one or more tests. Before you fix on your choice, it will probably be useful to double-check your findings against the following checklist:

- Do you have enough evidence that the test measures a key requirement for the job concerned? Has a proper job analysis or validation study been carried out?

- Does the test come with a manual that provides technical information and instructions for test administration?
- Is there an alternative form of the test in case you need to administer it a second time or one of them is compromised?
- Is there an objective scoring key?
- Is each of the scales measured statistically reliable?
- Is there evidence of validity for the type of job and population targeted?
- Are there published norms for the targeted job and population?
- Do you have someone trained to administer, score and interpret the scores?

Checking the standardisation, reliability and validity of tests
On Monday you learnt of the importance of norms, reliability and validity. These issues are especially relevant to the use of personality tests for two reasons:

1 *Personality tests are normative,* i.e. individual results are always scored by comparing them to the rest of the population. Quoting a score without referencing it to the general population or to some specific sector such as professionals or managers is meaningless.
2 *Personality tests are not infallible.* Unless we have some measure of their accuracy and their relevance to the issues we wish to explore, then once again we will be on shaky ground and in danger of misinterpreting the results. Even as a test user, we need to check out the three issues of norms, reliability and validity.

Norms

Employers using personality tests must be confident that the test is not subject to bias, or, where there is bias (e.g. sex differences), that any discrimination that does arise is real and justified in terms of the job itself.

Here are some guidelines on what you are looking for:

- *Size of sample:* this should be at least 1,000, evenly distributed between males and females.
- *Norm populations:* the overall sample for the general population should be taken from a wide range of organisations. Check the range of organisations used: a sample of three companies probably does not represent a balanced sample.
- *Specialised norm groups:* norm tables for groups closely related to your intended target should be provided.

Reliability

Most modern tests are very reliable in terms of the design of items, given the free availability of computer software for item analysis. However, you do need to pay attention to test–retest reliability, which is a measure of the accuracy of the test. Obviously, it is not sensible to use a test whose results can vary considerably.

Validity

The fact that a test has high reliability, i.e. that it produces consistent results, is no guarantee that it is actually measuring what the publisher claims it does (construct validity) or, more importantly, that it will provide useful information to the decision-maker (criterion-based validity). Ask yourself whether what you are seeing really matches what you are seeking in your organisation.

Using professional reviews

There are a number of sources of help in obtaining high-quality evaluative information about tests, and a number of these have been mentioned throughout the week. One excellent source is the British Psychological Society which publishes reviews of ability and aptitude tests, as well as of personality assessment instruments. These reviews consist of independent and rigorous test evaluations in common use. Each review consists of:

- test details
- general information
- administration and scoring
- documentation
- evaluation

They are a good source of both information and reassurance.

The interpretation of test results

There is a common perception that companies use personality tests to discover our weaknesses. Amongst cynics, the regulation of the use of tests is seen as a way of increasing their mystique and of sewing up the market. Whilst it cannot be denied that certain publishers use some restrictions for commercial benefit, the truth is that the restricted use of tests and the professional code of practice applied in the UK is ultimately for the protection of the user.

Here are four important rules for the use of personality tests that all test-users should follow:

- Rule One: the results of personality tests *must* be interpreted by a qualified and experienced expert.
- Rule Two: the results should normally be confirmed by a feedback interview with the respondent or through supporting evidence (e.g. peer reviews, assessment centres).
- Rule Three: if the results cannot be confirmed by other means, their significance should be reduced and treated with caution.
- Rule Four: only draw conclusions for those factors or qualities that have been shown to be important predictors of performance.

When interpreting results, we often find people suffer from misconceptions as to what the tests show. Here are some simple principles that are often ignored:

- There is no such thing as a right or wrong personal profile. Scoring high or low on one dimension is a measure not of how good you are but of how unusual you are!
- Extreme personalities are interesting to us, but so are typical or average scores on personality dimensions. Someone who shows an average level of assertiveness will generally seek to gain a balance between being preoccupied with getting the job done to achieve results (whatever the cost!) and adapting to changed circumstances, quickly finding new solutions.
- We can only talk about the degree of match between your profile and the job or circumstances you find yourself in.
- When there is a mismatch, people can experience discomfort or learn to adapt. An individual's natural preference is not the same as their observed behaviour.
- The words used to describe personality traits are often emotive in common language and need professional interpretation. For that reason, computer reports tend to read like astrology forecasts ('you may be inclined to … it is possible you may feel anger …').
- Everything is relative, including our own reaction to the results. The use of the label 'sensitive' or 'sentimental' simply means you will probably appreciate music, the arts, a film or book with a creative or emotive theme more than a practical hobby, an action-packed film, a detective novel or a biography.

Summary

The key points of today's discussion involve not just the tests themselves but also three other vital elements:

1 selecting the test or battery of tests appropriate to the purpose
2 defining and following a process to deliver the required results
3 reviewing and evaluating at every stage.

Tomorrow we shall look at some wider aspects of the uses of psychometric tests.

The uses of psychometric tests

Today we shall be reviewing the wider range of uses for psychometric tests within organisations. In doing this, we will consider:

- the range of uses for tests
- personal development
- team construction and team building
- other tests

The range of uses for tests

Psychological tests can serve a variety of uses in an organisation. In the coming pages, we shall consider some of the more important ones.

Screening and short-listing
By selecting this option, the management team is also deciding that for the job in question it would prefer to employ people with more developed skills in a particular area. The managers concerned need to be committed to the importance of the abilities in question, and candidates, on their part, will expect to be given a fair opportunity to demonstrate their potential.

In combination with other methods of assessment
Tests are probably best viewed as an integral part of the complete assessment of an individual, rather like examining the pieces that make up a complete jigsaw. They might be used, for example, to identify some key issues that can be explored in greater depth in a subsequent

interview. Alternatively, they may provide complementary evidence, confirming aspects of behaviour or competencies identified by other means (e.g. 360-degree surveys (see p 63), assessment centres).

The challenge for anyone interpreting results is to tease out the possible explanations for any inconsistencies in performance and to arrive at a reasoned and valid judgement about a candidate's true ability or personal disposition. Weighing up and evaluating psychometric results effectively requires experience and judgement, but in the right hands it leads to a more rounded and balanced evaluation of an individual's true strengths and weaknesses.

Placement
A detailed study of individuals using personality tests and questionnaires can play a valuable role in matching individuals to jobs that best suit them, thereby helping management to make optimum use of the human resources available to them.

Other applications
Creative managers can in fact identify many uses for
psychometric tests in the workplace.

- A newly appointed chief executive could use tests to
  handle sensitive issues relating to the senior manager
  group in a takeover or merger. Not only can they provide
  an insight into the nature of the team, especially if
  performance records/feedback are limited or missing, but
  they can also provide a source of information to support
  future decisions on deployment, promotion, development
  and outplacements.
- Tests can support initiatives to improve the quality of
  work performance in change or quality initiatives.
- In a company with sensitive industrial relations, the use
  of tests to identify the potential for retraining and job
  changes can significantly reduce the potential for conflict
  in the workplace.

Personal development

One of the most exciting trends has been the growing use
of tests to enrich an individual's insight into their own
capability, potential and development needs. Providing
individuals with professional feedback on test results in a
career counselling session allows them to gain a better
understanding of their personal qualities and to take
ownership of their own development process.

For the use of personality tests to be effective, a number of
conditions need to apply:

- Subjects need to be volunteers not conscripts

- The test instrument must have a good level of face validity
- Written reports are not as powerful as a feedback discussion with someone qualified and experienced
- Such discussions need to be developmental – i.e. what can I do now I know this?

Using psychometrics for development: a case study
At the Institute of Management, we have had great success with numerous organisations using a combination of tools for assessment. The chosen tools are:

1 *MSAT.* This applied judgement test has already been described (see p 38), and it provides objective data on the knowledge, judgement and critical thinking of subjects in the context of realistic management situations.
2 *a psychometric test.* This is usually a factor -based test such as 16PF or the similar 15FQ. It often provides the 'backdrop' or the underlying rationale or explanation for why people behave the way they do at work.
3 *a 360-degree assessment process.* This is a quantitative assessment based on a competence framework (either the organisation's own or one based on the Institute's own competence data bank). It involves polling up to 15 stakeholders, and provides a comprehensive quantitative picture of the behaviour of the subject as seen through the eyes of others.

The above is a comprehensive and thoroughgoing approach which is somewhat unusual in its scope and depth. However, for the individuals involved, the 'three-dimensional' data it provides is often the most powerful that they have ever received.

Because of the quantitative nature of the data, it is possible to aggregate it. This enables the data to be analysed using some sophisticated statistical techniques (e.g. factor analysis and cluster analysis). This in turn generates a very comprehensive picture at corporate level that encompasses competence, roles, culture and so on.

One of the conclusions that can be drawn from such experience is that, as with selection, psychometric tests work very well in conjunction with other data derived from different sources.

Team construction and team building

Questionnaires like the Myers-Briggs Type Indicator and Belbin's Team Role Inventory can provide considerable insight into the way a person interrelates with others, their preferred role in group situations and their favoured work environment. This can help members of a team to understand each other's strengths and weaknesses and to avoid dangerous blind spots in the way a team functions.

The Belbin Team Role Inventory
The Belbin Team Role Inventory is widespread in its use and recognition. In many organisations, the development that goes with certain levels of seniority is often accompanied by some consideration of the team roles. For this reason, and because of its high face validity, it is worth considering briefly the Inventory itself.

Dr Meredith Belbin, in his research on behaviour with people in group environments, suggested that there are eight primary roles which people adopt in teams:

The eight roles are:

1 *Shaper:* the driver of the objectives and priorities; the agenda setter; these tend to be dominant, dynamic individuals.
2 *Chairman:* this individual controls the way in which the team moves towards the group objectives; they make the team cohere; they tend to be dominant and dynamic.
3 *Monitor-Evaluator:* this individual analyses problems and evaluates ideas and suggestions; they are analytical, tenacious – a critic.
4 *Plant:* this individual is the ideas generator: creating new approaches; they are unorthodox, intelligent, imaginative.
5 *Team Worker:* this individual supports team members, builds the team spirit; they are diplomatic and sympathetic.
6 *Company Worker:* this individual translates ideas into action; they are stable, cautious organisers.
7 *Completer-Finisher:* this individual is oriented to the achievement of goals and the completion of tasks; they are disciplined and conscientious.
8 *Resource Investigator:* this individual is oriented to communication and contact with the outside world; they are extravert, enthusiastic and likeable.

There is a simple self-scored test that will help you to define your own preferred team role and team-role profile. It has proved very useful when members of a team discuss their own preferred team roles and how these operates in terms of the actual team processes.

The Learning Styles Inventory

Another framework, which also has a self-scored test instrument widely available, is the Learning Styles Inventory of D. Honey and A Mumford. This is based on the learning cycle of D Kolb, an American psychologist. Kolb said that learning is a cyclical process involving a number of components:

- Experience
- Experimenting
- Observation/Reflection
- Theorising/conceptualising

Honey and Mumford suggested that people have a repertoire of behaviours and preferences in relation to this learning cycle. That is, we have strengths and weaknesses, and are not all equally skilled at each of these stages.

The Learning Styles Inventory is a test instrument that gives a subject a profile of scores against four learning styles, so enabling them to identify their own preferred learning style. The four learning styles are:

1 *The Activist:* this is someone whose preferred style is to engage in new experiences. They enjoy getting involved in here-and-now activities. They enjoy the 'buzz' or risk of new activities.
2 *The Reflector:* reflectors like to take time, and think things through from various angles before acting. They are cautious and measured, and mull over information before reaching conclusions. They don't like to be rushed or pressurised.

3 *The Theorist:* this individual assimilates, integrates and synthesises information about the world into rational schemes. They are interested in principles, assumptions, objectivity and logic.

4 *The Pragmatist:* this individual values new ideas, not as an end in themselves, but to see if they work in practice. They are down to earth and enjoy getting on with practical activities and problem-solving.

THEORIST

REFLECTOR   PRAGMATIST   ACTIVIST

People who are engaged in development processes are often encouraged to test their own profile for Learning Styles. The Inventory has a very high level of face validity and has the benefit of confirming and reassuring people that their natural preferences for learning are sound. Thus, it can help them to make choices about the range of development activities that will suit their style.

It is also known that learning styles can be volatile, or at least sensitive to the changing context of the subject. The good side of this story is that people can change or develop their repertoire of learning approaches along with new experiences.

Other tests

The purpose of this book is not to provide a complete digest of all of the tests, or indeed of all of the test types, that are available. We would need many more than seven days to do that! However, we shall use this section to paint a picture of just some of the many other tests and classes that are available.

There is a class of tests that are used for research, clinical and therapeutic purposes and that have little relevance to organisational life. They are so specialised that we will not consider them here. However, there is another complete class of tests that we have not yet discussed, and these are tests that relate to values and interests. In fact, there are many such tests that give information about what people value and about life interests, going on then to relate this to interests in relation to types of career. An example is the work of Holland who classified career theme interests into the following categories:

- Realistic
- Investigative
- Artistic
- Social
- Enterprising
- Conventional

Here are some other aspects of personal and behavioural preference for which there are test instruments:

- selling styles
- management style
- conflict style
- creativity
- motivation
- stress
- leadership

And there are many more...

Summary

Today we have looked at the wider perspective of using tests. We have looked at the range of types of test available. In particular we have looked at using tests both for personal development, and for constructing and developing teams. We have suggested a whole range of areas within the context of working life where tests might be appropriate.

Finally, we have looked more specifically at a number of tests that have a very wide usage and currency in organisations:

- The Belbin Team Role Profile, and
- The Learning Styles Profile

Tomorrow we will widen our perspective to look at some of the organisational issues associated with testing.

The organisational perspective

Today, we are going to draw the threads together of all of the various aspects of testing that we have considered this week. For the most part, we have so far discussed testing within its own context. What we shall do today is look at it from the point of view of the organisation, and examine the implications for those responsible for the use of tests within organisations.

We shall look at:

- becoming an accredited user
- the ethical use of tests
- guidelines for using tests in organisations
- next steps
- a summary of the week

Becoming an accredited user

Once an organisation decides to use or develop psychometric tests, it has three options to choose from,

1 using expert advice
2 using a bureau service, or
3 developing in-house expertise.

Properly developed tests are only available in the UK to people who are properly trained in their use. If your company has no qualified staff to administer and interpret tests, it must buy in outside expertise. Of course there are many suppliers of psychometric tests who may support these with public and in-company training courses.

However, using the right expertise for the administration of tests is just the start of the process. It is far more important that your organisation give some thought to the best way to select, interpret and develop the applications involving tests. For this you need to build up expertise *within* the organisation and take ownership of processes. Choosing a reputable bureau service may seem a simple decision to take, but in the long term will that option automatically deliver the best decisions for the company?

Getting qualified
Although psychometric tests can significantly improve human-resource decisions, this can only be achieved by the competent use of these instruments. Inappropriate use can not only destroy the effectiveness of a well-thought out selection process but it can also have a damaging impact on the test-takers themselves. To gain the required level of competence, you need expertise in:

- selecting, administering and scoring tests
- interpreting the results in the specific context of the application for which they are being used
- appreciating the underlying statistics and methodology used to generate the results
- understanding the limitations of tests
- presenting complex information in the best form to decision-makers and test-takers

For this reason, access to psychometric test materials in the UK and many other countries is restricted to those who are suitably qualified. Organisations need to recognise the importance of this protection and should themselves take steps to ensure that all test applications are only handled by qualified personnel.

Even if you do not want to become qualified yourself, it is still wise to familiarise yourself with some of the key issues in test assessment before making any important decisions on the use of test materials. Without this grounding, you will not be in a position, for example, to critically evaluate and select tests from the growing number of tests available, along with the claims made by their publishers. Many providers offer short programmes on the basic use of psychometric tests. Even if you have received some form of general grounding, you may want to consider becoming qualified in the administration and interpretation of tests to the British Psychological Society's standards, i.e:

- the *British Psychological Society's Level A Certificate of Competence in Occupational Testing:* Level A covers the general foundations of testing, and the performance skills associated with test administration and interpretation for ability tests.

- the *BPS's Level B Certificate of Competence in Occupational Testing:* Level B complements Level A. It increases the scope of the scheme to include personality assessment. It covers the use and interpretation of personality tests. Level B can only be gained once you have gained a Level-A qualification.

If you have gained qualifications outside the UK, you may write to the BPS to have your qualifications recognised as the equivalent of Level A and B. As a user, you can also check whether experts are registered on the BPS register for qualified test personnel.

Finally, many publishers offer conversion training for the use of their own psychometric tests on the grounds that their instruments are sufficiently distinct from others to justify some form of test-specific training. This is a somewhat controversial issue in psychological circles as it is seen by some as a somewhat questionable commercial device to maximise return and impose some form of protectionism. Certainly, responsible, qualified experts can be expected to familiarise themselves with all aspects of a test which they are considering using.

The ethical use of tests

Most people tend to view uncertainty and change with unease and distrust, especially if it affects their job opportunities and careers. The user of tests has an important responsibility to recognise and deal with these natural fears, as well as to administer tests properly. The introduction of 'scientific' tests may well be met with negative responses from the work force. Those who have not studied recently may find them daunting and with no obvious relationship to the day-to-day realities of the workplace. Test users must take their responsibilities to the test-takers just as seriously as they do those towards the organisation.

Communication
Any user of tests must take special steps to provide adequate information to clarify and clear up possible misunderstandings. Without this buy-in, you cannot expect potential test-takers to participate willingly or sit the tests without the potential for unreliable results. The purpose of the tests, the way in which they are developed and applied, and the treatment of data must be explained to gain acceptance from the test-takers.

Candidate care
Before embarking on tests, provide the test-taker with adequate information regarding the use of the test, the procedure involved, the likely duration of the test and the

likely outcome of the assessment process. Offer guidance and support only in a way that is consistent with the test administration instructions and does not invalidate the process.

Equal opportunities and culture fairness
There are some very simple steps managers can take to promote equal opportunities:

1 *Evaluate the tests.* Check out the procedures used by the test developers to avoid insensitive content or language and to identify potential bias.
2 *Review the performance of test-takers.* Compare the performance of test-takers of different gender and ethnic origin when samples of sufficient size are available.
3 *Modify the test administration if necessary.* Where necessary and feasible, use modified forms or altered administration procedures for test-takers with disabilities. Where bias in tests has been demonstrated, identify the cause with the help of expert advice or consider scrapping the use of the test.

Test administration and scoring
The facilities used for testing are critical. Candidates must be provided with a quiet, well-illuminated and ventilated room, complete with properly spaced tables and chairs. The tests must be carried out under the control of a properly trained administrator and be free from any interruptions, otherwise the test results are invalidated.

Test feedback
As a general rule, you should take steps to ensure that test-takers are provided with adequate feedback from a qualified expert. Certainly, where tests are used in selection,

you must ensure that all candidates are treated equally. Avoid the temptation to treat internal candidates differently from external applicants because one-to-one feedback is expensive; if in doubt, make sure all test-takers are treated the same.

There will also be situations where it may in fact be ill-advised to provide detailed feedback. Providing too much insight into the assessment methodology might allow individuals to deliberately practise their skills in key areas and so lead to corruption of the process.

Security and access

All test materials should be stored securely, with access restricted to trained test users. Users should respect the copyright on test materials and inform publishers of any infringements that come to light. Ultimately, this is in the user's interest since any infringement of copyright will probably mean that the test might be corrupted by being passed on to the public.

Locked storage facilities, accompanied by proper company policies governing security and access to personal information, are a must for any test-user. Access must be strictly limited to those who genuinely need to know the test results. Test data must also only be used for the purpose for which it was intended and for which informed consent was obtained.

Lastly, any automated storage of results means that the individuals concerned have rights of access to the information under the provisions of the Data Protection Act. From October 1998, this includes non-electronic forms of systematic data collection.

Disposal

Most important, when the purpose for which the tests were used has been achieved, the user must ensure that steps are taken to dispose of any paperwork properly. Unfortunately, test results can all too often be retained far beyond their shelf-life.

Guidelines for using tests in organisations

Even the best test can deliver flawed information when it forms part of a poorly designed process. It is therefore good practice to establish a comprehensive policy on testing and to issue clear guidance to all those involved in the use of tests. Such a policy should identify:

- on what basis tests will be used
- who will take decisions on the use of tests

- who will have access to results
- how the results will be used and incorporated within decision-making processes
- how equal-opportunities issues will be dealt with
- the policy for confidentiality and providing feedback

Organisations like the Institute of Personnel and Development, as well as major publishers, can offer a lot of help in this area. Saville & Holdsworth issues a series of *Guidelines for Best Practice* in the selection and recruitment process.

Next steps

This book has equipped you with the basic information that should help you to separate between fact and fiction and should help you to understand more clearly how, as a manager or personnel professional, you can introduce tests into your organisation or use them more effectively. However, the use of psychometric tests is a complex subject, and we have only been able to review the main topics superficially.

Getting the best out of tests really requires managers to take ownership of the issue of test use, rather than delegating it to the Personnel Department. To achieve this, management teams need to become informed about all of the topics covered in this book.

We certainly hope that reading this introduction is just a beginning and that you may wish to cross the threshold into a deeper knowledge and increased ability to apply psychological tests. Some topics you might wish to explore include:

- assessing learning styles in your staff and accommodating these within your frameworks for training and development
- designing company-wide systems to help employees improve personal effectiveness
- using assessment or development centres to exploit and develop staff skills
- identifying the critical factors for success in your most effective employees, and perhaps separating between fact and fantasy

There are many ways you can increase your knowledge and understanding, such as:

- attending workshops and conferences
- reading books and journal articles on the subject
- joining or forming a discussion group, either by meeting or through the Internet
- discussing topics with your colleagues and friends
- joining a professional association with an interest in this area, to be informed of events, resources and new developments in the field
- writing to test publishers to gain more information about their instruments and support materials
- gaining qualifications in test administration and interpretation

Summary

Over the last seven days, we have covered a lot of ground on the use of psychometric tests in organisations. After this brief introduction, you should be able to:

- understand how psychometric tests are constructed and developed
- gain insight into what aptitudes and abilities can be tested and how
- be familiar with some well known and commonly used tests of ability and personality
- evaluate tests for use in selection processes
- understand some of the issues involved in using tests for other processes such as development and team-building
- understand some of the wider issues involved in using tests in an organisational setting
- know where and in what circumstances to seek further information and help

Useful addresses

The British Psychological Society (BPS), 48 Princess Road East, Leicester LE1 7DR. Tel.: 0116 254 9568, Fax: 0116 247 0787.

The Institute of Management (IM), Management House, Cottingham Road, Corby, Northants, NN17 1TT. Tel.: 01536 204222.

The Institute of Personnel and Development (IPD), IPD House, Camp Road, London SW19 4UX. Tel.: 0181 971 9000.

Test suppliers and publishers

Oxford Psychologists Press Ltd, Lambourne House, 311–321 Banbury Road, Oxford, OX2 7JH. Tel.: 01865 311353.

The Psychological Corporation, Foots Cray, High Street, Sidcup, DA14 5HP.

Psytech International Ltd, The Grange, Church Road, Pulloxhill, Beds, MK45 5HE. Tel.: 01525 720003.

Saville & Holdsworth Ltd, 3 AC Court, High Street, Thames Ditton, Surrey, KT7 0SR. Tel.: 0181 398 4170.

The Test Agency, Cray House, Woodlands Road, Henley on Thames, Oxon, RG9 4AE. Tel.: 01491 413413.

Further reading

BPS (1989) *Psychological Testing: Guidance for the User*, Leicester: The British Psychological Society.

EOC (1988) *Avoiding Sex Bias in Selection Testing: Guidance for Employers,* Manchester: Equal Opportunities Commission.

Gael S. (1987) *The Job Analysis Handbook for Business, Industry and Government,* Chichester: John Wiley & Sons.

IPD (1993) *The IPM Code on Psychological Testing,* London: The Institute of Personnel and Development.

Pearn, M. & Kandola, R. (1988) *Job Analysis – A Practical Guide for Managers,* London: The Institute of Personnel Management – now IPD.

Smith, M. & Robertson, I. (1993) *Advances in Selection and Assessment,* Chichester: John Wiley & Sons.

Further *Successful Business in a Week* **titles from Hodder & Stoughton and the Institute of Management all at £6.99**

0 340 71205 8	Appraisals in a Week	❏	0 340 70541 8	Planning Your Own Career
0 340 70546 9	Assertiveness in a Week			in a Week ❏
0 340 57640 5	Budgeting in a Week	❏	0 340 70544 2	Presentation in a Week ❏
0 340 720778	Business Growth in a Week	❏	0 340 71208 2	Process Management in a Week ❏
0 340 71199 X	Business Plans in a Week		0 340 70539 6	Project Management in a Week ❏
0 340 59813 1	Business Writing in a Week		0 340 64761 2	Problem Solving in a Week ❏
0 340 71200 7	Communication at Work in a Week	❏	0 340 56479 2	Public Relations in a Week ❏
0 340 62032 3	Computing for Business in a Week	❏	0 340 62738 7	Purchasing in a Week ❏
0 340 71196 5	Customer Care in a Week		0 340 71198 1	Report Writing in a Week ❏
0 340 70543 4	CVs in a Week	❏	0 340 70538 8	Selling in a Week ❏
0 340 63154 6	Decision Making in a Week	❏	0 340 67397 4	Selling on the Internet in a Week ❏
0 340 62741 7	Direct Mail in a Week	❏	0 340 71201 5	Stress Management in a Week ❏
0 340 64330 7	Empowerment in a Week	❏	0 340 70542 6	Succeeding at Interviews in a Week ❏
0 340 66374 X	Environmental Management		0 340 72076 X	Successfully Dealing with
	in a Week	❏		Difficult People in a Week ❏
0 340 71192 2	Finance for Non-Financial		0 340 71207 4	Teambuilding in a Week ❏
	Managers in a Week	❏	0 340 70547 7	Time Management in a Week ❏
0 340 71189 2	Flexible Working in a Week		0 340 71195 7	Training in a Week ❏
0 340 67925 5	Fundraising and Sponsorship		0 340 71197 3	Understanding Benchmarking
	in a Week	❏		in a Week ❏
0 340 71204 X	Going Freelance in a Week	❏	0 340 70540 X	Understanding Business on the
0 340 65487 2	Human Resource Management			Internet in a Week ❏
	in a Week	❏	0 340 62103 6	Understanding Business Process
0 340 59812 3	Interviewing in a Week			Re-engineering in a Week ❏
0 340 71179 5	Intranets in a Week		0 340 56850 X	Understanding Just in Time
0 340 63152 X	Introducing Management in a Week	❏		in a Week ❏
0 340 71203 i	Introduction to Bookkeeping		0 340 71173 6	Understanding Management
	and Accounting in a Week	❏		Gurus in a Week ❏
0 340 71202 3	Leadership in a Week		0 340 71174 4	Understanding Mind Maps®
0 340 65503 8	Managing Change in a Week			in a Week ❏
0 340 63153 8	Managing Information in a Week		0 340 71123 X	Understanding Neuro-Linguistic
0 340 70537 X	Marketing in a Week			Programming in a Week ❏
0 340 67924 7	Marketing Plans in a Week		0 340 61888 4	Understanding Quality Management
0 340 57466 6	Market Research in a Week			Standards in a Week ❏
0 340 60894 3	Meetings in a Week		0 340 65504 6	Understanding Statistics in a Week ❏
0 340 61137 5	Mentoring in a Week		0 340 71191 4	Understanding Total Quality
0 340 57522 0	Motivation in a Week			Management in a Week ❏
0 340 70545 0	Negotiating in a Week		0 340 62102 8	Understanding VAT in a Week ❏
0 340 64341 2	Networking in a Week		0 340 67905 0	Understanding Virtual Organisation
0 340 72073 5	Personal Investment in a Week			in a Week ❏
0 340 67922 0	Planning for Retirement in a Week	❏	0 340 70508 6	Web Sites in a Week ❏

All Hodder & Stoughton books are available from your local bookshop or can be ordered direct from the publisher. Just tick the titles you want and fill in the form below. Prices and availability subject to change without notice.

To: Hodder & Stoughton Ltd, Cash Sales Department, Bookpoint, 39 Milton Park, Abingdon, Oxon, OX14 4TD. If you have a credit card you may order by telephone – 01235 400414.

E-mail address: orders@bookpoint.co.uk

Please enclose a cheque or postal order made payable to Bookpoint Ltd to the value of the cover price and allow the following for postage and packaging:

UK & BFPO: £4.30 for one book; £6.30 for two books; £8.30 for three books.

OVERSEAS & EIRE: £4.80 for one book; £7.10 for 2 or 3 books (surface mail).

Name: ....

Address: ....

....

If you would prefer to pay by credit card, please complete:

Please debit my Visa/Mastercard/Diner's Card/American Express (delete as appropriate) card no:

❑ ❑ ❑ ❑ ❑ ❑ ❑ ❑ ❑ ❑ ❑ ❑ ❑ ❑ ❑ ❑

Signature .... Expiry Date ....